-1-

I watched the twilight raindrops speed up on the windshield like silver comets rushing toward distant stars, outwards in thousands of paths, simultaneously repeating without end and out of nowhere. Where one raindrop flew to the top edge of the windshield, so another one chased it instantly. So many and rapid were these dots of rain that the glass stayed soaked.

The rain show reminded me of the people that have been on this earth. Families had children, merging lives with each other, sometimes travelling faster and farther than the family member before. Some others seemed not to move from their location. So many people have lived on our planet with so many origins and directions in their lives like the movement of these raindrops. Each one belonged in a bubble in time, but all were part of the same human race.

My mind led me back to work and the people I had seen today. Those clients let me see into their lives and came to me for help with trust in a stranger. I wished they had everything they needed and didn't have to ask, but we didn't live in that world or time. I saw families all day at Social Services (DSS) who needed help feeding their families. They asked for Food and Nutrition Assistance, otherwise known as Food Stamps, which were monetary benefits that are paid out on a plastic debit card (EBT card), each month.

Just as the raindrops pushed the others up and outward, similarly, many parents, grandparents, guardians, aunts, and uncles did the same: raised the children and encouraged them to make their own ways in the world as they moved through life. As one client from earlier that day said to me,

"I want my son to do better than me."

This mother who just had her fifth baby, living in a single-wide mobile home that was not even big enough to house the husband and brother of this client along with all of her children. She said she was too afraid to call the police on her neighbors who sold drugs in the park. Her 18-yr-old son was a customer of theirs, and this mother wanted him clean. She said he did not speak English but had a work authorization card. I told her about where he could find jobs and how she could get help for him without attracting attention to herself around the neighbors. I mentioned where she could get free diapers and made sure that she had WIC, which was a supplemental nutrition benefit for pregnant women and children under five. She nodded and thanked me for the diaper information. I also asked her if she had applied for her three school-age children to have free breakfast and lunch at school since it was the start of a new school year, and she said yes. Her brow increased a bit as she thought about her predicament, but then her face relaxed. She seemed relieved as I finished up her food stamp recertification paperwork, which she submitted every six months when it was due, as that fed her four youngest children, who were citizens. We finished up our conversation and paperwork transaction quickly, as I keyed the final approval and stated her benefit amount with a reassuring smile. I told her to keep looking forward and to take care of herself and her family. She said may God bless me in her language.

She noticed that her milk started to leak and got up to hurry home, as she lived a 25-minute drive from the office. As I walked her out to the closed lobby, which was completely empty at this time of day, I had hoped to see a car waiting for her in the parking lot. I watched her leave, and through the glass doors I could see her cross the street and wait at the bus stop for her ride home. She looked up at the sky that was beginning to rain. I wanted to offer her a ride so that she would not get wet and could get home faster to feed her baby, but that was forbidden by the agency for food stamp workers. We were not allowed to do any favors for clients nor have contact with clients outside of the agency. We were not allowed to give out bus passes to clients who had come to the agency to renew their food stamps. Pre-stamped envelopes were mailed to clients with their recertifications and applications, so clients did have the option to mail in and did not have to appear in person. Many clients chose to appear in person, as occasionally a recertification or accompanying paperwork disappeared in the mail.

As I walked to my car, I thought about my client and her family. I hoped that her life and her family's lives would get better. Maybe she could get her son off drugs. Maybe the sheriff's department would sting the drug-pushing neighbors. At least they could buy food. All I could do at that point was hope for them.

-2-

W hen I started working at DSS I didn't have much to do for the first three months. Online webinars on case management were short, lasting 30 minutes each, and a class here and there on login and password instruction filled up almost half of a day. A three-day orientation with management on local government policy and procedure was a highlight , I was able to meet others working in different departments and other government officials. Once that was over, my job ,along with a few others on my team, was to change the caseworker's name in the case to match an alphabetized list according to clients' last names. I didn't know it at the time, but those caseworkers were not working their alphabetized lists. They were working other caseworker lists and seeing clients for other caseworkers. I wondered if this was the type of work I would do day after day, which seemed meaningless. I had applied to Social Services to help clients directly, so I said nothing and continued to key in names, hoping one day to make more of an impact.

After three months of data entry on changing names, the Food Stamp training class began. There were several team members in my class, and the days bled in and out monotonously with reading policy aloud from the government manual as we took turns. The second week, paper budgets designed by the government helped us calculate benefits for sample families. The trainer had invented case names such as Ned, Nellie and baby Nancy. No live cases were used to teach us how to process cases for real families while we were in training. I seriously doubted I would ever come across a family with those three names. There was no instruction on how to talk to clients, to comfort them and encourage them. Those interpersonal skills that had been listed in the job advertisement were "experience working with the public and needy families." I had no idea I would become a type of cheerleader or counselor when I was given a caseload as clients poured out their life story or latest financial or emotional predicament to me. I had approved and rejected health insurance applications in another state a few years back but did not have direct contact with clients in person as a caseworker. I did have 15 years of working with people in various office settings and customers. I had also lived in a homeless shelter for six weeks when I first moved to the town I lived in, so I did have some experience seeing those who suffered from different socio-economic problems. Little did I know that my past as a temporary homeless person from years back would make me empathetic and helpful to clients, but it also sharpened my skills sniffing out a lie. I had gotten to know many truth-tellers and good people at the homeless shelter, and I also met some who were not.

After training our team returned to our desks to complete "live" cases for client families on the computer. Our trainer performed "second party" reviews on the cases we completed up to the point where two mouse clicks were left to renew the six months, or in some cases twelve months, of food stamp benefits. Second party reviews were when the trainer checked our data entry, budgets and policy application to make sure the cases were correct before the clients received funds. Once the case was corrected by the caseworker and was approved through second party, the caseworker completed the case payout, and the client's EBT (food stamp card) was loaded with benefits on the client's designated payout date. Benefits paid out by the last digit of the Social Security number (SSN) on a certain date. For those without an SSN, benefits paid out of the third of the month. SSN's that ended in "1" also paid out on the third of the month, SSN's ending in "2" were paid out on the fifth, and so on until the 21st, where a final digit of "0" would pay out on that date. Tax ID numbers were not used as identification for undocumented (not having documents proving legal residency) clients. Undocumented clients could be a client of any race or national origin.

Clients were also known as "caseheads", or the person under who's name the case was listed. Undocumented caseheads did not have all their income counted, as they were not eligible to receive food stamps. A percentage of their income and their shelter expenses (such as rent or mortgage) were counted in calculating benefits for their documented (having documents for legal residency) or citizen children. For example, a family of four with two undocumented parents working and three documented or citizen children, would have the income added up, divided by five and multiplied by three so as to count the income for the children only. The same would occur with shelter expense. Certain types of income, including disability, and shelter expenses were counted for documented and citizens. Phone, utility expenses, childcare, and child support payment expenses were countable in Food Stamp cases. Medical expenses were counted for specific clients. Car insurance and other expenses such as clothing or gas were not counted. Drug felons had specific rules on receiving benefits, and some were banned from Food Stamp benefits for life if the felony was a certain class.

Bobbleheads resembled family members on the computer screen, with each family member's name listed below. The bobbleheads were faceless, but their names stuck with me. I was used to following ordinary rules of pronunciation in English and Spanish, but that changed for many names. I learned to ask a client on the phone how to pronounce a certain name when discussing family members with non-traditional names. Seeing eight to ten bobbleheads on a case now and then blew my mind since I only had two other family members. I enjoyed seeing the completed cases showing a determination of a few hundred dollars, or even over $1,000 for a month's worth of food for a large family. That was a great help to them and comforting to me since I knew they were struggling to make ends meet. Smaller families, or those with an income reaching up to the maximum allowed received smaller amounts.

Food pantry lists were given out in addition to WIC brochures for families to provide additional food resources. SNAP was another name for Food Stamps and meant "Supplemental Nutrition Assistance Program." Food stamps was the name commonly used in our agency. They were supplemental, meaning that if someone was earning or receiving income, benefits were designed to provide food assistance after that income was counted as a means to buy some food. It was never meant to be the sole source of buying food. Some were grateful and acknowledged the help as a relief, and some clients reacted to this indignantly as news to them. Resources such as bank accounts, additional vehicles, and other money were not counted on recertifications, but they were taken into consideration for new applications for food stamps. Regular food stamps were renewed every six months, and certain renewals were due yearly. Caseworkers were required to interview clients yearly via phone or in person. We sent appointment letters to the clients before addressing any income verification. Clients had several days to report for an interview or answer the phone. If a client missed the interview for the recertification, the case would close at the end of the month.

Once a client interviewed, and proof of income, if there was income, was not provided, the caseworker issued a letter asking for verification and if needed, shelter expenses. The client had a few days to return the verification, such as paystubs or a letter from the employer or income source. If the client did not return income verification within a certain period of time, the case would close at the end of the month. Sometimes clients returned a recertification late, such as the month after it was due. In that case, the caseworker needed to screen the client for expedited processing of benefits or issuing benefits if there was an urgent need for benefits and asking for verifications after processing. Again, the client needed to return verifications requested by another date, and if he or she did not, then the case would close. Closed cases could be reopened in certain situations, and in others, the client would need to reapply as a new application.

Caseworkers had various ways of verifying income sources beyond asking the client. Online computer applications provided specific details on earnings or receipt of income. Many times, I could process a case just by looking at the recertification, online verifications, and expense verifications from the past that had not changed. This was helpful, since caseloads numbered in the dozens and were "due" by a deadline. Caseworkers had certain days that they were visited by clients and did not process cases, since the visitors were one after the other. This meant that the caseworkers were doing "coverage" for other caseworkers since many times a caseworker did not see his or her own clients according to the alphabetized list. A caseworker would get a notice from the lobby check-in personnel to take a client, who was identified by a number only in order to protect his or her identity, to the caseworker office to conduct an interview and check the recertification paperwork to make sure it had been completed and signed. We scanned documents that clients handed us. Occasionally clients emailed us the proof of income and expenses. Those who did not have jobs and were able to work were referred to a job counselor on site.

When I first started working at Social Services, there were Food Stamp workers, childcare benefit workers, Medicaid (a medical benefit program) and other program workers seeing clients who requested these benefit workers to discuss cases. Then, after some time, the caseworkers were required to handle Food Stamps and Medicaid in the same visit if the client wanted to discuss both. The caseworkers were known as "Universal" since they handled more than one case. The object of this move-in procedure was to make the agency a "one-stop-shop" for clients so they would not have to repeat the same information over and over for each program. This caused enormous chaos since the caseworkers who had been doing Food Stamps for many years learned Medicaid policy and procedures and were expected to do both caseloads by a deadline in addition to visiting with clients who were not theirs. When a caseworker visited with a client who was not in their alphabet, the caseworker was expected to send the verification and recertification to the caseworker assigned to the case for processing when he or she was not seeing clients also. This also caused confusion for the clients, as many clients would ask, "Are you my worker?" We were not allowed to say that we were not the assigned worker. We were told us to say, "Yes, I can help you." Many clients would ask why they had a new worker each time they came to the agency and why there was a different worker name on the recertification paperwork they had just received, since it was different than our names. There was never a good explanation for that.

After a few months of processing cases I started to get a rhythm in processing quickly. I was able to keep up my quota of 80-100 cases per month simply by going paperless. I decided instead of printing out the recertifications, which were 4 pages long, and budgets (spreadsheet calculators issued by the state to determine benefits), I opened them online and scrolled through, entering numbers as needed. On days I visited with clients, I ended up skipping my 10-minute breaks in order to cram in a case to process. Some cases ended up taking 30 minutes to an hour depending on the number of family members and the different sources of income. When we were not seeing clients, caseworkers were allowed to use their headphones to listen to music on their phones. I found my music to energize my casework to help me focus, and this in turn enabled me to complete my casework quickly and accurately. I met with my manager often to ask for more cases once I had finished my caseload so that I could help other caseworkers. We were graded for quality on a number of cases each month.

Some families had self-employment income, which required a year's worth of verifications if we didn't already have the first six months' worth from the last recertification. Adding weekly, sometimes daily income and subtracting receipts for an entire year's worth of data was tedious, but I enjoyed it, as I could "zone in" and focus on accounting them. We could take client statements on earnings; however, if there was any evidence that showed up that indicated there was a credibility gap, I could refer the case to the Program Integrity department (the fraud investigators) for further handling of verifying aspects of the case.

Occasionally there would be a meeting where the entire Food Stamp department would gather and receive tips and feedback from management, and it was good to see other caseworkers who sat in different parts of the building. We spent most of our time in a cubicle, so meetings were a welcome relief. The agency also catered a hearty lunch twice per year, which included more than enough food for the various departments. Caseworkers chit-chatted over baked chicken and barbeque. There were smiles all around during those lunches. Four years later, Economic Services at DSS began to give away door prizes at the luncheons. We also started a social committee who sponsored pancake breakfasts, Thanksgiving potlucks, and other holiday festivities for the workers in all programs. I felt like I had found my new work "home."

We lost a kind soul that year. A Food Stamp caseworker who was everyone's favorite left too soon. He always had a grin on his face, and when I approached him the first month of handling cases to give him paper verifications for one of his clients that I had seen on coverage, he was appreciative. He lit up the room when he entered meetings, as he had many friends at DSS. One Saturday morning of overtime that I had volunteered for along with many other caseworkers, he had been expected but didn't show up. Monday morning, then Tuesday came along, and still no word from him. Finally, on Wednesday some caseworkers approached his manager and asked for a call or a visit to his home to check on him, as they said this was unlike him and were worried. We received terrible news the following day. He had died in his home while getting ready for work that Saturday morning. DSS was hit by a deep sadness that day, and a normally loud office floor became suddenly quiet once we found out the news. Each year on his birthday, those who remembered him wore red to commemorate his favorite college team. We never forgot his happy face and kindness.

There was a lot of comradery among caseworkers. Birthdays were celebrated by a decorated cubical and lots of cupcakes for the birthday person and the team. The late afternoon before a birthday, a caseworker or two could be seen hurriedly blowing up colorful balloons and hanging streamers in a coworker's cubicle for the next morning's surprise. Baby showers glittered the breakroom after work every couple of months, and the wonderful email full of good news to welcome a healthy baby boy or girl brightened our in-boxes a few weeks later. News of new hires along with a photo welcomed our coworkers into the fold, and they were also recognized in our biannual meetings. Those who had completed five to thirty years of service were also recognized in the meetings with loud applause and whoops and hollering. Even the death of a family member of a coworker was announced via email, and a sympathy card was passed around for signatures. Retirement celebrations ensured plenty of cake for everyone along with a congratulatory hug from attendees. The compassion was unlimited among caseworkers. I passed by offices occasionally on the way to the mailroom, and I overheard many caseworkers giving encouraging words to clients in distress. We were caring people, and it showed everyday with clients and with each other.

-3-

The first December at DSS I decided to give a little extra to special groups of clients. Another caseworker in our benefits department, which was known as Economic Services, had sponsored a group of nursing home residents that lived down the street, and DSS caseworkers were donating toiletries, socks, and other essentials so that she would deliver them on behalf of the agency. The Social Work department asked for donations for clients in the custody of DSS, as they were folks who did not have family to take care of them or needed Social Services to care for them; they were mostly adults. Even though we were not to have contact with clients outside the agency, I took the first caseworker's cue that I might be able to take on a special client visit, since hers was supported by the Director. I donated to both of those causes and decided to work on my own donation program. I supported all the residents of a recovery house, who's six ladies and their children used their benefits on the house food stamp card. They went shopping as a group, and the house management kept track of how much each client spent of their benefits as the card was used at the grocery store. This kept the clients from selling an EBT card. The ladies completed requirements in order to receive Food and Nutrition benefits. If they did not, then their babies received the benefits. The recovery house assisted pregnant women their young children that had been born while the mothers were in the program. Many of these clients no longer had family contact for one reason or another. Many of them had been in jail and were recovering from heroin addiction. As part of the program, these ladies no longer had contact with friends from their addiction past. They were beginning a new, clean life in a strict program. The house had a yearly talent show to raise money to keep the house running, and the clients had Medicaid to assist with medical treatment costs. I wanted to give these ladies encouragement and something special to open on their holiday since they would not receive gifts or have money to buy gifts. I knew I would need the support of the Director and made an appointment to run it by her.

My meeting with the director resulted in good news. She stated that I could do the donations as long as DSS's name was not tied to the donations. It had to have been a private donation. I felt encouraged that I could start a holiday gift drive for the house! Excitedly, I let my supervisor know, and she allowed me to invite my six other team members to donate, but she said we could not invite anyone outside the team to participate. The house director sent me a list of necessities, and my coworkers donated some funds. I received about $50 in donations, and it covered baby and adult toiletries at the dollar store. About two weeks before Christmas I spent half of my paycheck at Rose's department store to get more items from the wish list. Leggings, boots, sweaters, and other clothing items were wrapped and ready to go a few days before delivery.

I invited a caseworker from my team to go with me for the delivery. She was a sweet older lady with a soft voice who always presented herself with a great deal of patience. When we arrived at the house, I was nervous, since I hadn't met a lot of the ladies in person. Mostly I just knew them by the name under their bobblehead on the computer. My caseworker friend instantly put everyone at ease, as she picked up the first baby from her highchair and began to coo to her. We all sat on comfy couches, and my caseworker friend played with baby after baby on her bouncy lap. The living room where we sat was unlit, so it was a bit dark, but I could see the encouraging signs on the walls. Some of the inspiring plaques read, "One Day at a Time" and the serenity prayer, "God, grant me the strength to accept the things I cannot change, the courage to change the things I can, and the wisdom to know the difference."

The ladies were grateful for the gifts and thanked us for our kindness. We met more cute babies, and I tried to remember everyone's faces with their names so that I could see their faces in my mind the next time I processed their benefits. They had been through a hard life so far, but the comforting fact was that the babies were all healthy after some treatment. Almost all the babies had been born addicted to heroin, meth, or some other drug.

The second year of the gift delivery I had more help. My family friend, the owner of a local shop, found out that I worked at DSS and offered to donate for holiday gifts. I let my supervisor know that I was partnering with a local business to do the donations this time, and she smiled and agreed with my plan. The house director sent another enthusiastic wish list, and this time it had some high-dollar items on it, such as ipods and gift cards. Before sending the list to the company owner, I removed the high dollar items since those could be sold in exchange for cash. While I waited for the gifts, I invited a different caseworker from my team to accompany me. The company owner arrived with her SUV full of beautifully wrapped gifts in shiny holiday paper, marked with initials of the clients, that I transferred to my car for delivery. Only caseworkers could enter the house for this event due to keeping the identities of the clients and children confidential. This time I brought snacks, treats, and sodas to enjoy during our visit. This was a new group of ladies and babies, since the program was only a year long, and almost all the previous residents had graduated to start their new, independent lives as sober and clean mothers. The ones who had not graduated had moved out and had moved on. Some of them disappeared completely from our recertification lists once they left the house, as they did not apply for food stamps on their own. Some of them had their children taken away from them due to the mothers returning to addiction.

The caseworker and I held the sweet babies and chit-chatted with the mothers. We also met two volunteers who took care of the babies all day while the mothers were in recovery meetings or doing other tasks related to their program. The volunteers and the Assistant House Director were mothers and grandmothers themselves, and their calm demeanors showed that they had become experts in working with different types of people. The caseworker I brought said she wanted to see everyone open their gifts, and in order to save her face, I didn't say anything. I thought, "What about opening the gifts on the holiday? There won't be anything left to open." I smiled as the ladies tore into their packages. They were delighted to see beautiful, colorful outfits for the babies from Carters, foot spas, wool coats, toys, books, and other quality gifts. This year I saw more smiles. The dark living room lit up with happiness, and the House Director took our group photo. When the caseworker and I left, we said that we felt like we made another difference in clients' lives. I thought about them on Christmas Day as my husband and I opened gifts and knew they were enjoying theirs. I received individual thank you notes from the ladies at the house and shared them with my family friend. The authentic gratitude written in those notes showed progress in each woman's recovery.

The third year I decided to do the holiday gift drive I was supporting the men's recovery house more actively in addition to the women's house in the Food and Nutrition program. The state had a new policy where the caseworker in charge of the house EBT card was to do two site visits per month to check to make sure residents receiving benefits were still residents of the houses. The visits were always pleasant and short, as I arrived, met with office staff there, and left with lists of current residents in hand. The Director, office staff, and residents always thanked me for taking care of their food stamp needs. I felt welcome and when I returned to the agency after each visit, I felt rejuvenated in doing my casework.

I wanted to include a different group to help me with both recovery houses. One of the county's five-year goals that had just been published was to fight opioid addiction. I thought of the opportunity to invite the social fraternities and sororities at the local university to help with the donations. I met with the recovery House Director to see her reaction to my plan. She gave it 100% support and offered to do a house tour and discussion of the program to any groups that participated. I told my supervisor of my plan, and she said it was fine. August of that year I mailed letters to 30+ social Greek groups to invite them to participate, as I stated I was a Food Stamp caseworker doing this on my own and not behalf of DSS. I had given them the deadline of September 30th to let me know if they wanted to participate in the holiday gift drive. Hurricane Florence came to our town soon after mailing the letters, and I didn't hear back from any of the students, as the university had shut down for several weeks. Finally, in late October a sorority contacted me and asked if it was too late to participate. I was thrilled that someone had responded! Immediately, I welcomed them to join the donation drive. A week later I received an email from a fraternity who also offered to donate. Once I had the wish list in hand from the women's recovery House Director, I sent the list to the sorority, with initials instead of names. The men did not have a specific list and said any donations would be welcome. I let the fraternity know that in addition to toiletries, it might be nice to buy a long-sleeve shirt for each client at the men's house since it was winter, and those shirts would be useful, especially if they were sweatshirts. There were 12-15 men, and the fraternity agreed, so I contacted the house for the men's sizes.

I let both Greek groups know that in exchange for their donations, they would be invited to a house tour, as appropriate for their gender, while residents were out, and a discussion of the program. This event in turn would enable students to share the information about addiction and recovery with their other group members and possibly other students within the university, since fighting opioid addiction was one of the county's goals. Since the

Greek system was so numerous in population at the university and focused on community service projects, I thought this would be a great way for students to learn how addiction ruins people's lives and what life is like in recovery. I felt this would be a good deterrent for addiction so that students might think twice before becoming addicted, so as to avoid becoming parents who must go through recovery to take care of a newborn or to return home to take care of other children.

About a week later the fraternity dropped out. I didn't receive a specific reason in the email from them, so I let it go. I decided to ask my family friend if she wanted to buy the shirts for the men's house. She was enthused and got right to work on the gifts. I went to the dollar store and purchased toiletries, winter gloves, and hats for the 15 men. I had inherited some money from my generous grandmother who had passed away earlier that year. As I shopped, I felt that familiar comfort I had felt the Christmas prior when I visited the women's recovery house. As I approached the checkout, I had two carts filled with items, and customers behind me looked at them with curiosity and a look of concern that I might take a long time in checking out. I told the folks in line behind me quickly of my plan to give them as gifts during the holiday to residents in the recovery houses. I said it wouldn't take long, and that I would probably checkout quickly. A gentleman and his wife from the back of the line came forward and handed me $20 and said, "God bless you and what you are doing." My eyes welled up, as this elderly couple had touched my heart, but I smiled and said, "Thank you so much, this is really appreciated."

The holiday gift deliveries were on separate days for the men's and women's houses. I coordinated with the women's recovery House Director, who was the director for both houses, as well as the sorority which day and time would be best so that residents would be out of the home attending their group meetings. I didn't invite another caseworker to accompany me that year, as I had been moved a few months earlier to a team that focused on two other programs in addition to Food Stamps. There was no way to take the other coworker in my group from her desk, even for a few minutes. She was seeing my clients and hers during my visits to the houses. I had ordered BBQ and chicken lunches for the women's house this time and went to pick them up to leave them for the residents when they got back after their meetings.

A silver Mercedes pulled into the driveway slowly at the women's recovery house, and as we opened the front door, two excited 20-year-old ladies walked in with gift after gift. The large sedan was filled with gifts that also packed the trunk. The two sorority members were all smiles as they brought in more and more items. Diaper boxes, clothes, toys, and other needed gifts entered the house as if it were Santa arriving himself. Santa with a Mercedes sleigh! The House Director and Assistant Director thanked the visitors profusely and asked the ladies about their studies. As they spoke, I could see the sincerity in their faces and the dedication they had to helping people. I knew that when they graduated, whatever career they pursued, they would be helping others. The sorority exceeded our expectations, even though we should not have had expectations. The House Director described the program and gave the visitors a tour of the rooms. They were all so grateful, as their faces told that they had never seen a recovery house for mothers and children before. The volunteers holding babies came out of the nursery room to greet the sorority members and thank them. I left before the visitors finished their meeting at the house but thanked them on the way out and told them that they made a difference in these ladies' and babies' lives. Returning to the office, I felt that familiar warm sparkle in my heart.

The day of the men's gift delivery I went to pick up the KFC dinners for the men. I arrived at the house after work since I wanted to visit with them. My family friend had put an extra wrapped gift with each shirt so that the men had a little more to open than just a shirt. I brought in the wrapped gifts, toiletries, and some of the men carried the food to the kitchen. The House Director brought all the men who had returned home from work into the parlor. The house had been a funeral home in decades past, and its elegant high ceilings still bore the decorative carvings. The interior windows still housed the beautiful antique stained glass. The stone fireplace was enormous, and the hardwood floors squeaked when folks walked from room to room. Plastic chairs lined the walls of the parlor, and men began to sit quietly. The Christmas tree stood proudly in the front corner window. It must have been 10 feet tall, and on it, among the glittering lights, hung paper ornaments with the names of all those in the community who had donated to the recent drive for financial assistance to support the house. The men who lived at the recovery house were not eligible for Medicaid to pay for treatment unless they were on disability, so many of them did low-wage work in order to pay their rent at the house. It was hard for many of them to find a good-paying job since drug felonies and other criminal history barred many from some employment. There was a grace period before they were charged rent, but that time passed quickly. These men were juggling recovery expectations set by the house program and a job at the same time, and many of them succeeded, as they graduated. Almost all the men were back in the house from outside, and they focused their eyes on the House Director as she introduced me. She asked me to say a few words, and since I had not anticipated this, I felt a little nervous.

Quickly my thoughts returned to my grandmother, who had left me some money, and what I didn't use to pay my bills, I had used to buy some of the gifts. My grandmother Joan, who had always helped alcoholics and drug addicts during her life, I felt was standing beside me to give me the words to speak. Joan, who had preferred that I use her name instead of grandma, had also worked at DSS in another county for decades. She was a British GI bride who had met my grandfather Jack during WWII in England. After moving to the U.S., she had worked as a secretary, then became a caseworker and then received her promotion to supervisor. She even received the Order of the Long Leaf Pine, which was the highest award given by the governor for service, back in 1988. In her personal life after my grandfather died, she dedicated much of her personal time to take care of alcoholics in our family and drug addicted friends. She never fell to addiction herself, even though I saw her with a glass from time to time but remained a strong and steady rock for those who needed her when they were suffering. She gave rides to others who needed medical appointments, phoned those who felt lonely, donated money to many charitable causes, and even housed an addict or two in her large home.

I thanked the group for having me and told them of my generous family friend who had bought the larger gifts for the men to open on their holiday. I recounted how my grandmother had always thought of others and cared for others who were suffering due to addiction. She had never shared where she worked with me, and it was only in her obituary handed out at the funeral that I learned of her dedication to Social Services. I spent more time with her after she retired and remembered her giving rides, encouragement and donations to those who found themselves struggling with addiction. I told them that I felt her standing beside me in spirit, and that she would have wanted to help them too. The men's faces had a look of peace and understanding. Some of them smiled at me, and some got up to shake my hand. As I left the house that night and drove home, I couldn't help but yell, "Yes!" with a fist pump from joy at the two holiday deliveries. These had been chances to give a little extra to others in need.

-4-

V isits from clients renewing their Food Stamp cases became more meaningful as time went on. I learned to listen and empathize with my heart and sensitive words as clients poured out their stories. Many grandmothers, grandfathers, and great grandmothers were primary caregivers to the children in their homes, and they shared their financial hardships with me as if I were sitting with them in their living rooms. I will never forget the grandmother who began to cry when she told me how much she missed her husband who had passed away the past year. She said they had 43 years together, and that she missed him every day. She showed me a crinkled photo of them together from many years ago. They looked so in love and happy, smiling from a time past when they didn't know that one would leave the other suddenly. We cried together. We couldn't help it. As we dried our tears, she said that her grandchildren kept her going, and that she protected them with everything she had since they lived in a high crime area. She was living on Social Security and some cash assistance the agency had given her monthly. The Food Stamps were critical, as they ensured the free phone service for her "Obama phone," free breakfast and lunch for her school-age grandchildren, and to cover some of the food that the teenagers in her home were consuming rapidly. As we finished processing her recertification, and I ensured her benefit amount, she stood up and gave me a hug and whispered "Thank you" in my ear. We looked at each other and smiled teary smiles.

I realized from visit after visit how much the folks on Food Stamps and myself differ from those who were not struggling financially. What I mean is that those who come into the agency asking for help were having the worst financial period of their lives hit them in the face. There was a single grandfather who was taking care of his three grandsons, and he was working full time in general labor. He did not have any assistance beyond food stamps, and looking at his paystubs and his rent receipts, I really didn't know how he got by each month. His attitude was phenomenal despite his financial situation, as he remained positive and focused during each interview to renew his benefits. I could tell that he was raising his grandsons with a tough but loving force. Many of my clients were proud and did not want to ask for help. Many clients said they would rather work hard or just "get by" with their Social Security and pensions than ask for handouts. This was especially repeated by the older generation of caretakers. Due to the increased cost of living and the pressure to give the children in their homes the latest fashions or technology, they came to DSS for extra help in feeding their loved ones, as money ran out quickly each month after paying bills. Many of these caretakers told me that they had already raised children, and here they were raising children again. They told me they loved their grandchildren, nieces, nephews, and wards that they were raising, but they hadn't expected to do this again at their age. Many parents of these children were in prison, drug addicts on the street, had the children taken away due to neglect, or had disappeared altogether. I wondered how the divide had happened so drastically between the economic classes. Many of my clients had worked their whole lives at jobs, yet they lived in poverty. Those who were not struggling financially I determined to be the ones who could afford "expensive" houses, as I saw those online in the available real estate section of my local listings. Most house purchase prices started at $200k, and the ones near the beach closest to my home started at $1M. The average rent for a two-bedroom apartment started at around $900 per month. Some other towns had homes for less, but some of my clients would not be able to afford those either.

Sometimes families came in together. Often mothers, fathers, children and babies all crammed into my cubical to ensure their benefits would stay in place or increase. I had some stuffed animals, a couple of kids' toys, markers and worksheets to keep the older children occupied. They enjoyed showing me pictures they had drawn and wanted to leave them with me to remember them by. This was especially touching since they were thoughtful. The families who came in as a group always made sure to tell the kids to clean up when I let them know I was finished entering information, and this made me happy. Some of the kids who, became bored watched as I entered information into the computer. They were fascinated by the signature pad, which was an electronic device upon which a client could sign his or her name to agree to the terms of benefits. I told the children who wanted to play with it that if they behaved and cleaned up that they would get a chance to sign their names. True to my word, I closed the real computer application and let the children sign their names into a fake document. They were delighted in thinking that they had a part in the business at hand that their parents were doing. Every now and then I saw a child run out of another caseworker's cubical and down the hallway, and a parent bolted after them frantically. I had a few of those too. It made the day interesting when we had a "runner."

Repeat client visits to my office were my favorite, as I could remember their last visit and asked them about a recent surgery they had been planning since our last visit, or how the children were doing at the new school they were attending. I got to know some clients well during those visits, and that made my job fulfilling. Yearly increases in a Food Stamp benefit amount were always met with a relieved sigh and a positive comment. When I had to deny a recertification due to a client with too much income, I knew that it would be hard on that person. Most of the time, when a client made "too much" money, most of the time it really wasn't a lot of money. It was barely over the threshold, and somehow this client would have to figure out how to juggle the loss of a benefit in trying to cover all expenses in the household. When I realized due to income or policy that a client would be denied for a recertification while he or she was sitting next to me in my office, I gave the news personally before the automated system sent them a generic letter in the mail. That way a client could plan a budget before getting the bad news in a cold letter. I showed them the calculations and let them know they could reapply at any time the next month should their situation change. I also gave them food pantry information and encouraged them to go to one. Many reacted with panic, as they stated they needed their benefits desperately, and I told them that I was sorry for the outcome. Some became really angry and started yelling and cursing me. I never yelled back, and we had two deputies on standby in the lobby to screen for weapons and to assist employees with clients who got out of control. When I had an angry client, my caseworker neighbors in adjacent cubicles would message me in chat and ask if I needed help or a deputy. I tried to deescalate the situation most of the time with empathy. The one time I did need an authority figure in my cubicle doorway to speak to a client, the deputy calmed her down, and she left quietly.

-5-

The phone rang off the hook one March Friday afternoon, and my cases were backed up. I juggled answering questions from clients on the phone with finishing up the last few cases that were due by the following Monday's deadline. I wasn't on coverage, so I had spent the day working like a silent worker bee. I had five more cases to finish after lunch and felt sure that if there weren't any computer application problems, I could probably get them all worked.

I picked up the ringing receiver and greeted a gravelly Southern woman's voice. She explained that she was waiting on her Food Stamp benefit amount since she hadn't gotten her approval yet in the mail. Her impatient tone demanded to know how much she was going to get in benefits. I verified her identity by her SSN, checked her case, and it was one of the cases in my path for that afternoon. I asked her if she minded holding for a couple of minutes since I thought I could process the case quickly. An indignant sigh followed the yes, and I put her on silent mode. I ran the online verification to double check any income that might have been reported by the state's Economic Security Commission, which showed new earned income that had been reported by an employer. There was a "hit" that showed her husband had a new job that had started a couple of months prior. I took a look again at the recertification paperwork she had sent in, and there was no income listed at all, and for the question about anyone in the home starting a new job had an X by the block marked "No." I got back on the line with the client.

"Ma'am, I will have to call you back in a few minutes. I apologize, but there is an issue I will need to take care of."

She sounded annoyed but asked me to call her back right away. I called the place of employment and asked to verify the employee's status there.

Over the loud clanking of dishes and conversation, the voice on the phone said, "Oh, yeah, he works here as a manager, but you'll have to get his salary from the owner who's not here. I'll give you his number."

I called the owner, and after letting him know that I needed the wages quickly since this was urgent, he agreed to email them to me right away. I was surprised that the owner did this so quickly since most of the time I was met with voicemail when I called anyone from the County's phone. The emailed showed enough income to put the client's family over the limits for benefits. The client's husband was earning $5K per month gross (before taxes) with a family of three, and the rent was not marked on the recertification. There were no other expenses to count against the income. It looked on paper as if the family was living on nothing at all and didn't have any bills.

I called the client back and asked her if her husband was working at the location. I didn't tell her yet that I had already verified. What if he had quit the night before I verified and didn't tell the owner yet? Her voice changed into a frantic low-growl. "No-o, uh, uh, he ain't workin'. He's NEVER worked there." I informed her that I had already spoken with the owner who verified his income. I gently let her know that her case was over income since she hadn't marked any expenses I could count against the income. Her voice changed again to a high-pitched squeaky growl and she asked me to hold on for a minute. There were muffled voices, and then she returned to the phone.

"Um, when I said my husband wasn't workin' there, well…he is. I couldn't say anything before 'cause he was in the room with me. He don't even give me no money anyway. Our marriage is bad. I don't ever hardly talk to him."

I replied, "It's okay, we have to count his income, but if your situation changes, you're welcome to reapply."

She wasn't ready to let go yet, as she spoke more quickly and more franticly. "Like I said, our marriage is real bad and I have no money. What do I need to do to get my son and I some benefits? Do I need to have him move out? What should I do?"

I was not about to tell this client what to do with her personal life, but based on my previous experience with giving bad news, I needed to tip-toe on this call. Gently, I said, "Ma'am, I am sorry, but I can only take information that is given to me and process based on what I receive from verifications. I can't give you marriage advice. I'm sorry."

"I DON'T NEED MARRIAGE ADVICE!" she snapped. "I don't like what you just said. I think you thought I lied about my husband workin'. WHO is your supervisor?"

I told her my supervisor's contact information calmly. She ended the call with a non-gravelly, pleasant voice as she thanked me and told me to have a great day, which I found to be strange, since I hadn't heard this cheerful voice from her before. At that point I knew I needed to let my supervisor know the backstory, but she had already left for the day. I was pretty sure this client's voicemail to my supervisor would be heard before my conversation with the her on Monday morning.

Monday morning, I tried to talk to my supervisor before she checked her messages. I told her the story, and she nodded quickly, expressionless, and returned to her computer screen without comment. I wasn't sure what the nod meant since it was as if I had just told the story to my cubicle wall.

That afternoon my supervisor said that I needed to meet with her to do some coaching. I knew it. I was getting written up. When I entered the conference room, my supervisor and my former supervisor where there to document the conversation. My supervisor's take on my call with the unhappy client was that I should have asked if she were in danger since she had to cover up the fact that her husband was working. I thought, "Ok, I missed that point, but it doesn't deserve a write-up." Then my supervisor advised me that when the client asked what she should have done to get benefits, I should have told her how much in benefits she would receive if she had her husband move out and that she would receive full benefits, as his income wouldn't count."

I said, "What? It sounds like I should have told the client how to work the system and now I am trouble because I didn't." I also thought, why would I tell a client to have her husband move out? Wouldn't that be her friend or her therapist's responsibility?

My supervisor responded that no one would see the coaching and that signing it only showed acknowledgment but not acceptance of what was written. I signed it. Not signing it would have meant insubordination, and I wasn't about to head into firing eligibility.

A few months later this "private" coaching appeared on my yearly employee review that was submitted to the County's HR office.

-6-

A fter I left DSS a couple of years later, the clients stayed in my heart. I thought about them all the time. The year before I resigned, a grocery store and a strip mall that had other neighborhood businesses burned down near our agency. Most of the neighborhood residents were struggling financially, and many of them were receiving Food Stamp benefits. Families who had walked to the grocery store just down the street and ate breakfast at the café in the same shopping center now had to walk a mile and a half in the other direction. The closest grocery store and place to eat a cooked meal were a far walk on the side of a major road with heavily-traffic and no sidewalk. For some who had income, those clients could take a bus to the store or even an Uber, but many residents did not have the luxury of travelling when their money ran out. Travelling on foot at night or in inclement weather was impossible, as it was too dangerous. There had been crime reports in the neighborhood, and a gang was present. Families did the best they could with the Family Dollar that was near our agency. It was the only store within a reasonable walking distance besides a gas station. The burned lot sat vacant month after month. I visited one of the apartment offices to find out any news about whether the lot would have a grocery store again. The office staff told me that a management company had bought the lot and that I could contact them to ask. I called the said management company and left voicemails and emails. No response. I decided to do something about it. I wrote a petition that I published on Change.org and took around to various neighborhoods and downtown to get support for the rebuild of the grocery store. I also called two county commissioners, and one of them agreed to send a letter to the management company to ask them to consider rebuilding. I removed the photos of the persons from this copy of the petition:

Kelsi Arcos started this petition to a management company and City of Wilmington

On May 2, 2018 at 7:16pm, Village Plaza, located at 1022 Greenfield Street in Wilmington, North Carolina burned down. What remains is a dirt lot. Everybody's IGA supermarket, Spiro's Breakfast and Lunch House, Quails Quality Cuts barber shop, and City Life Church all disappeared. Residents in the neighborhoods of Houston Moore, Village of Greenfield, Lake Forest, Garden Lakes, Jervay, Hillcrest, and Glover Plaza are no longer able to purchase fresh food and prepared meals in their neighborhoods, as they had relied on these businesses that were located a reasonable distance from their homes. Residents of these neighborhoods are having to walk 1.5 miles to the nearest grocery store, Food Lion on Oleander Dr., in order to purchase produce, meats, or other prepared foods and meals. The residents of the neighborhoods of Creekwood North, Creekwood South, and Rankin Terrace have to walk over 3 miles to the nearest grocery store, which is also a Food Lion, on Market St. Many residents are having to rely on assistance payments to get by in addition to holding jobs to feed their families, so money is scarce with regards to transportation. The local Social Services Agency cannot provide transportation vouchers to get food. All of these neighborhoods are food deserts, and they are all in neighborhoods that do not have economic development.

The United States Department of Agriculture defines a food desert: "To qualify as a "low-access community," at least 500 people and/or at least 33 percent of the census tract's population must reside more than one mile from a supermarket or large grocery store," per the website americannutritionassociation.org. The convenience stores and Family Dollar stores nearby are not carrying fresh meats, produce, and other nutritious foods that the residents need. Many residents who cannot afford bus transportation or other means of getting rides to the nearest supermarket are walking, often in boiling hot sun or freezing temperatures, in the rain, or in dangerous evening conditions with children having to walk alongside them in order to purchase groceries and meals. Returning home after having walked the same distance but now carrying heavy grocery bags, and many times with an exhausted toddler or two struggling to keep up, is too much to bear for these residents. The only other source of assistance for fresh produce are the food pantries located around town, or the Local Motive Mobile Farmer's Market, run by Feast Down East, that only operates during Wilmington Housing Authority hours of 8:30-4:30 Monday thru Friday. The mobile farmer's market stops at each neighborhood once per week for a two-hour *period to sell produce from local farms, such as eggs, strawberries, collard greens, etc. This farmer's market is not able to provide the same service that a regular grocery store can provide for residents in these areas.*

A management company purchased the land at Village Plaza November 2018 but has yet to make public its intent on rebuilding the much needed grocery store and restaurant. Messages were left on the management company owner's voicemail on April 24 and May 8th asking the status of the rebuild of Village Plaza, but none of the messages were returned. The "contact us" form was filled out on April 25 on the company's website and submitted asking for the status of the rebuild, but no answer was received. WECT News broadcast a story on April 23 regarding Village Plaza as well and also contacted the management company for a comment with no response per their news website. This petition is to ask the management company and The City of Wilmington to work together to rebuild grocery stores in these food deserts that will sell fresh food and prepared meals. These neighborhood residents deserve the dignity and convenience of being able to purchase fresh food and meals to feed their families. The photos shown are of what remains today of Village Plaza, a family who are expecting a baby purchasing from the mobile Farmer's Market, the Farmer's Market setting up at Houston Moore, a resident of Greenfield Village who needs the grocery store to buy her great granddaughter nutritious food, and two homeless men (the one on the left is a veteran who has lost his leg) who have to travel from the homeless shelter in the Village of Greenfield area to Food Lion to buy food. Please sign this petition to help us get the message across to The City of Wilmington and the management company to get grocery stores in neighborhoods that need economic development. Thank you.

Various residents in the neighborhoods helped get signatures. We did not knock on doors, as we did not want to disturb anyone, but asked folks in the street passing by for support. Some drove up to us in their vehicles to sign, and some businesses had everyone working at that moment sign as well. We did not take donations since it was not our land to use. The barber shop had moved a few streets over, but the employees who signed the petition were happy that we were trying to get the neighborhood back on its feet. All who signed the document were eager to get the grocery store back in the neighborhood. The television station interviewed me, and I told them that we needed economic development in the Greenfield neighborhood. It was located next to a beautiful lake and an amphitheater. I had imagined once the strip mall was rebuilt that the neighborhood would have more of a community feel. Everyone in downtown could have benefited from the grocery store, as there wasn't one. All economic levels of residents could have shopped there, since it was a little more than a mile to the river where historic homes stood and new apartment lofts had just been built.

I signed up to speak to the City Council in May 2019 to present the petition since they handled permitting issues and had televised meetings. I sent a copy of the petition to the management company. I was nervous, and my friend who had helped me get signatures stood beside me to speak as well. We only had five minutes, but we jam packed it with determination and details of the reality of how folks who live in food deserts struggle. I was extremely nervous but mentioned my history of working with clients who lived in the neighborhood and the meeting with a local grocery/restaurant owner who I tried to persuade to open an additional location on Greenfield St. My friend, who said did not want to be mentioned after the meeting, told the council about her struggles with transportation costs to travel to the closest grocery store. There was enough of a population as future customers; we had the entire downtown, with residents in all economic levels to support the grocery store since there wasn't one within miles. The infrastructure was there: a paved parking lot, lights, electrical lines, sewer, etc. After about two weeks, a representative from the management company called me and said that the grocery store would not be profitable, and that the management company's family had already done enough charity for our town. I told him that we were not asking for charity. We were asking to rebuild a business that was desperately needed in the community. I asked him what the company's plans were to do with the land since they purchased it six months after the strip mall burned down. The representative said he didn't know but maybe he could sell it back to the county or the city and they could build a grocery store.

I went back to speak to the City Council for a second time in June to let them know what I had been told by the management company. A local grocery store/restaurant owner had rejected the idea of opening in the neighborhood. He had another restaurant planned in a more affluent neighborhood near a Walmart. I asked the City Council to contact the management company and ask them to consider building affordable housing instead if they were against rebuilding the grocery store. I reminded them of the working poor who were the backbone of our city, as they did jobs that were needed every day. There was no reaction visually nor in writing from the City Council.

I sent an email to the Mayor and copied the county commissioner who had written a letter to the management company. I also copied the reporters at the local newspaper. Finally, I got a call from the Mayor who said that he called the management company, and the rep said they would be happy to rebuild the grocery store. That it was never an issue, but that they would need for a tenant to be found first. The Mayor suggested that I find a business to be a tenant who would sign a contract with the management company. He said I was so good at being socially active that I probably would be able to do it.

I had no money, no title, and no power. How was I supposed to get a grocery store to move into a building that hadn't been built yet that sat on a burned-out lot and I didn't own the land? I called several grocery store chains and emailed others. Only two returned my messages. One grocery store chain, who was the most responsive, said I would only need three things: permission from the nearest franchise with that same name in a town 20 miles away, a store manager with experience running a large supermarket, and $800k to start. The newspaper reporter contacted me, and I told her how this would need to be a community effort and that we needed a government or a business leader to help us conquer this food desert to help this community. I didn't have the financials or expertise to fund this.

Often, I think about my former clients who receive food benefits and know they are doing the best they can to keep food on the table for their loved ones. At the time of this writing the lot on Greenfield St. stood vacant. All I can do is hope.

www.ingramcontent.com/pod-product-compliance
Lightning Source LLC
Chambersburg PA
CBHW030424160726
47992CB00007B/3267